OCEAN FRONT

THE STORY OF THE WAR IN THE PACIFIC 1941-44

ONE SHILLING NET

Pearl Harbour . .

OCEAN

THE STORY OF THE WA

London : His Majesty's Stationery Office, 1945.
Price 1s. 0d. net. S.O. Code 70-462*
Printed by Harrison and Sons, Limited, London

This book tells the story of the war against Japan on the sea and island battlefields of the Pacific and in the skies above it.

It is the story of a great war : vast in its distances, for the whole stretch of Europe from Lisbon to the Urals is shorter than the ocean span from Tokyo to Pearl Harbour ; imposing in the magnitude of the forces engaged ; long in duration, for it is now in its fourth year.

It is the story of an intensely dramatic war, opening with the shattering treachery of Pearl Harbour, the stroke which in one morning gave Japan command of the Central and Western Pacific ; then moving on to the long Allied holding action—the battles of Coral Sea and Midway, the nerve-racking struggles in Papua and Guadalcanal to stave off Japanese victory. Its climax is the astonishing Allied counter-offensive : the slow, painful beginning in the Solomons and New Guinea ; the quickening pace ; the sudden reappearance of the United States Pacific Fleet, striking due west from Pearl Harbour like a giant restored, breaking open the Japanese island

THE WAR SPREAD 5,000 MILES FROM NORTH TO SOUTH, 6,500 MILES FROM EAST TO WEST.

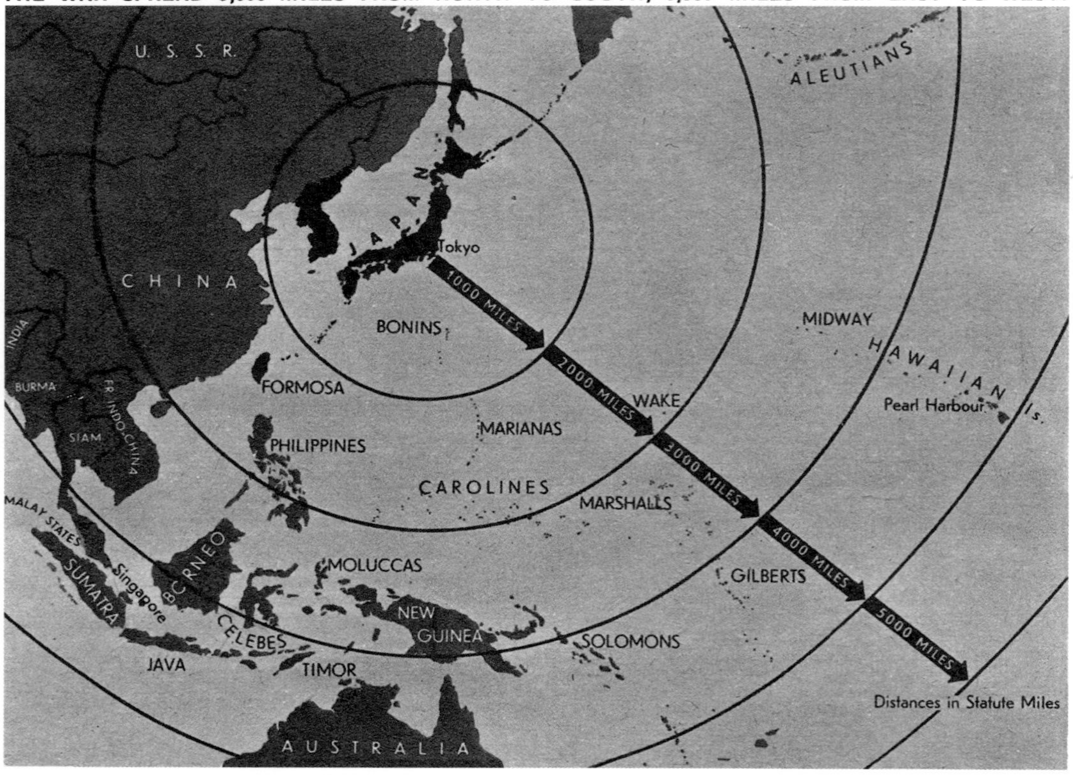

ENEMY FORCES FANNED OUT FAST. THE MAI

FRONT

IN THE PACIFIC 1941-44

ISSUED BY THE
MINISTRY OF INFORMATION

. . December 7, 1941.

empire ; and then, with all the parts falling into place, the invasion of the Philippines two and a half years after the surrender of Bataan.

It is the story of a war fought against the most romantic background in the world : the swaying, tropical palm trees, now gashed, splintered forests ; the quiet islands, now ravaged by bomb and shell ; the blue lagoons and white beaches, now stained with blood ; fought to the south in the steaming jungles of New Guinea, to the north upon the black and freezing Aleutian outposts.

But one essential part of the long front against Japan is not touched in this book—the war in Burma, where the forces of South-East Asia Command, primarily British, are fighting the campaign that has become one of Japan's largest military commitments. That story is told elsewhere. In this book, issued by the British Ministry of Information, the story is of Americans, of Australians and New Zealanders, hardly at all of fighting men from Britain. It is a book dedicated to those who fight far away from the main British forces : 12,000 miles away, yet close by their side.

JAPANESE GAINS WERE MADE IN 90 DAYS.

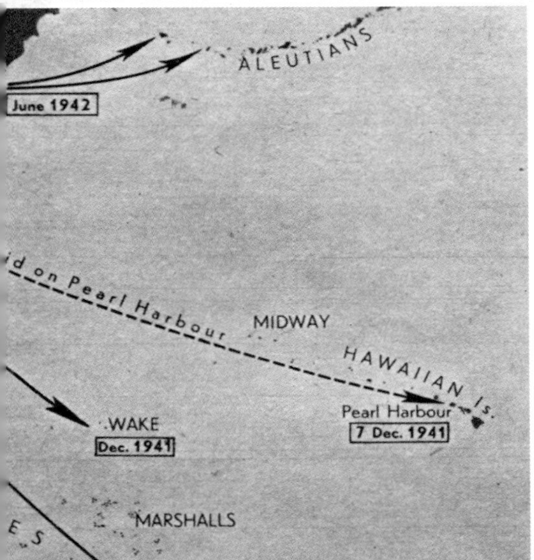

THE DEEP ALLIED ADVANCE FROM THE OUTER TO INNER LINE IS THE STORY OF THIS BOOK.

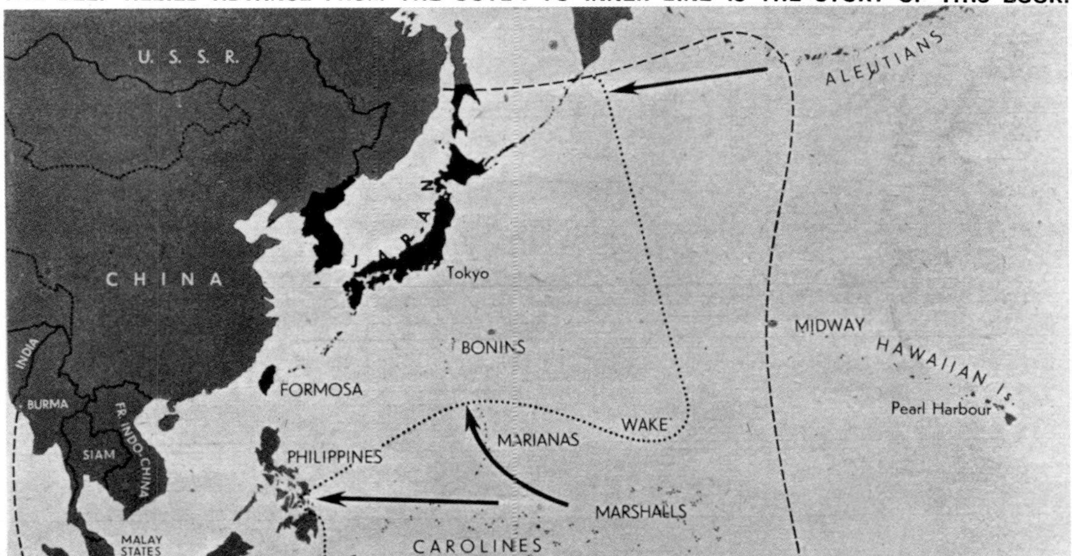

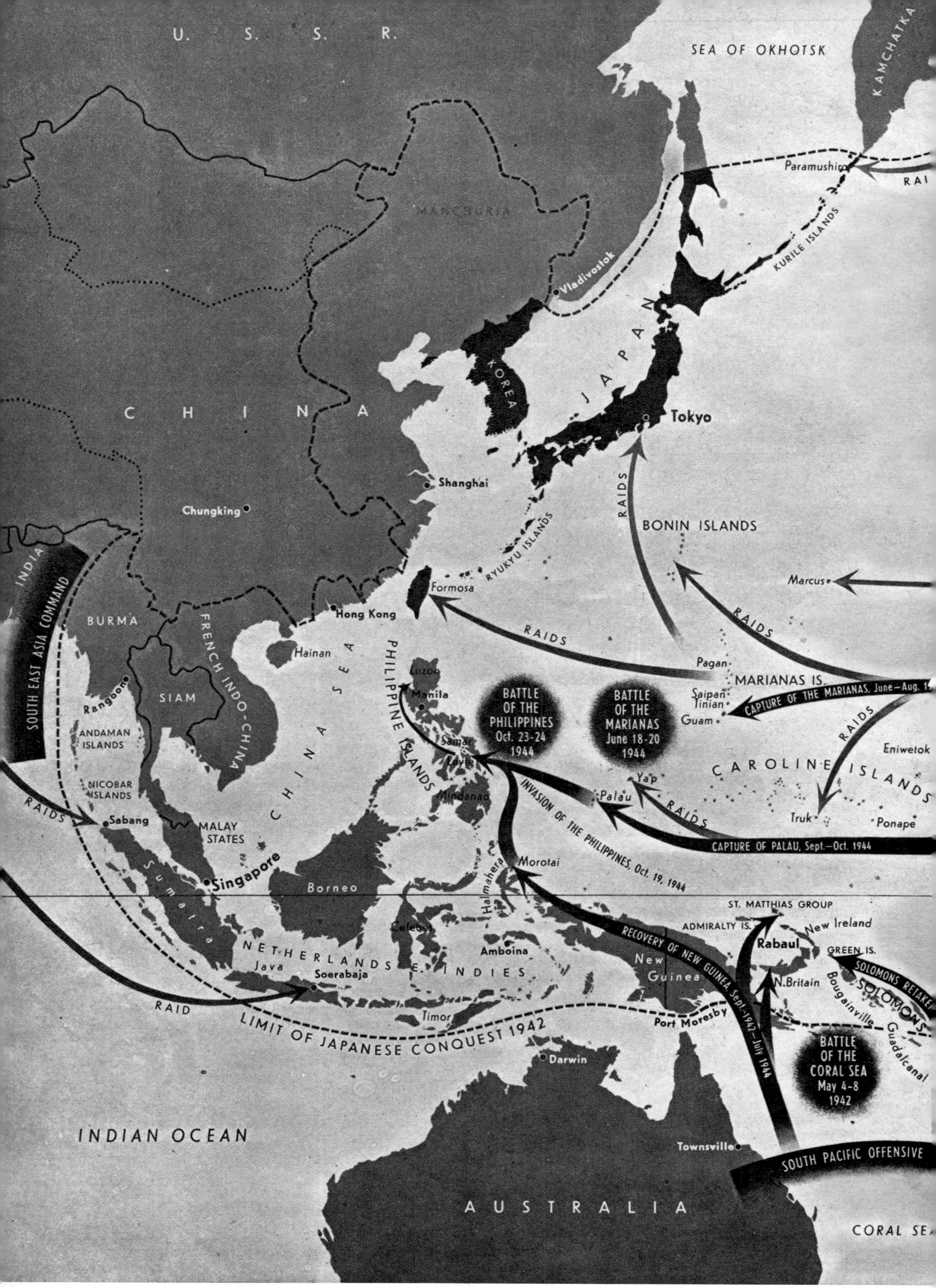

The path of the Allied offensive in the Pacific from August 1942 until the invasion of the Philippines in October 1944 is shown here. Black arrows trace the movement of the advancing forces. Main air-sea attacks ahead of the land forces are indicated by the lighter grey arrows. The broken line represents (approximately in China) the limit of Japanese conquest in 1942. The offensive began in the south, simultaneously in New Guinea and the Solomons. Notice how it bends towards its objective, the Philippines, from its starting point 2,000 miles away. A year later the United States Fleet opened

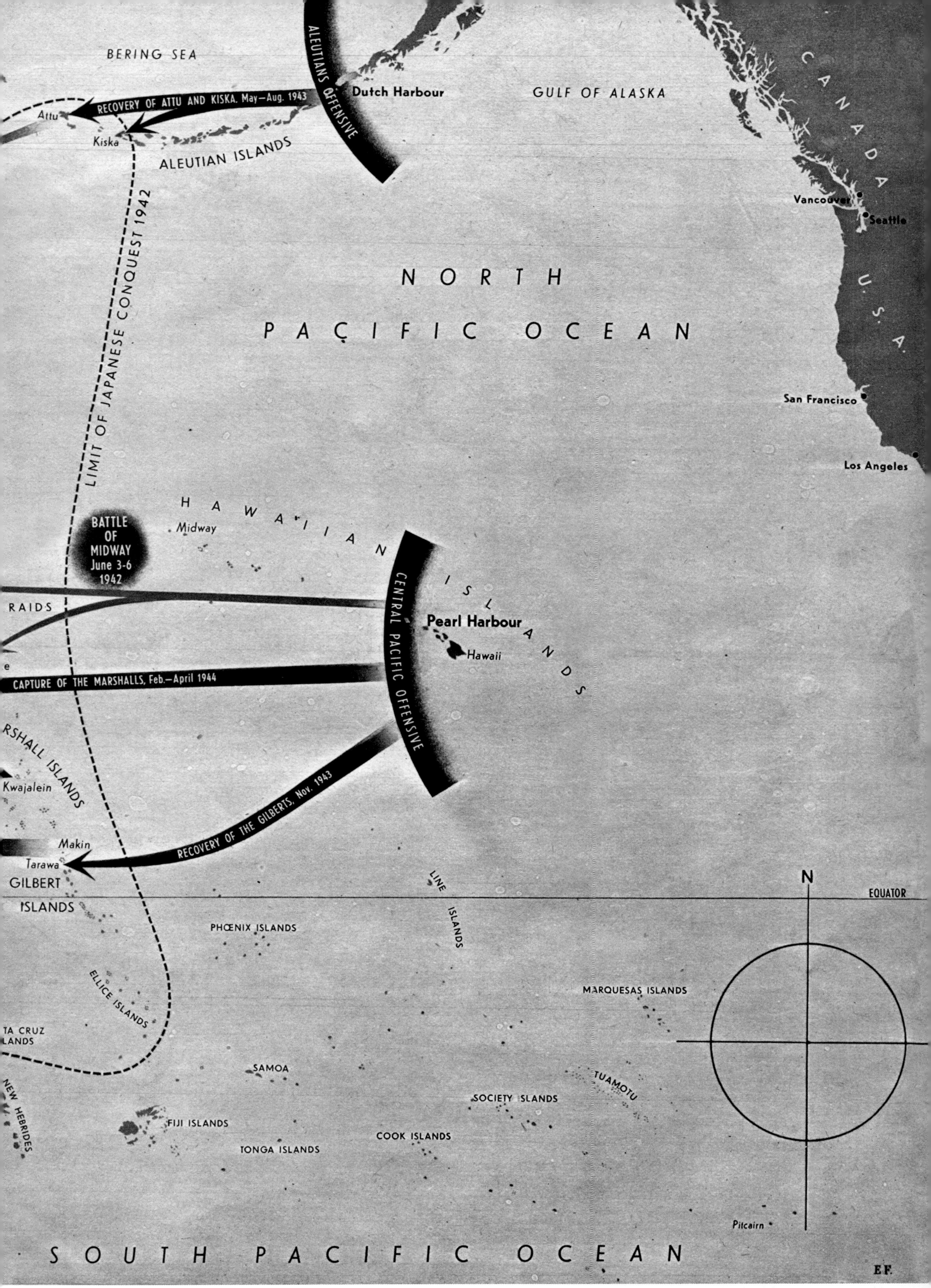

its tremendous offensive from Pearl Harbour, striking west, also towards the Philippines. As 1944 progressed, these two offensives—MacArthur's from Australia, Admiral Nimitz's from Hawaii—converged, until by September, with MacArthur in Morotai and Nimitz in Palau, they had cut through the heart of Japan's island empire, and were poised together for the united attack on the Philippines. Once so marked on a map, the widely separate movements of the Pacific war emerge as a closely concerted plan for the recapture of the Philippines, strategic key to all Japan's overseas conquests.

BLACK CLOUDS FROM SHELLS HANG IN THE NOISE-FILLED SKY AS AMERICAN SHIPS DEFENDING MIDWAY BEAT ASIDE JAPANESE BOMBERS

1. THE TURNING POINT: CORAL SEA AND MIDWAY

The Battle of the Coral Sea was fought on May 4th-8th, 1942, the battle of Midway a month later, June 3rd-6th. These two air-sea battles finally blocked the Japanese advance along the whole ocean front. They were the Pacific turning point. They saved Australia and New Zealand from direct attack. They protected for good and all Pearl

FROM CARRIERS 200 MILES AWAY. THE YORKTOWN, TARGET OF THE ATTACK, HEELS OVER IN A VIOLENT SWERVE. THIS IS OCEAN FRONT.

Harbour and the Allied line of communication from the United States across the S.W. Pacific to the bases of eastern Australia.

The map on the preceding page shows where the Battle of the Coral Sea was fought. On May 6th, the Japanese fleet steamed south from its bases in the New Guinea and New Britain area. It was breaking fresh water. Its probable immediate goal was Port Moresby, Australian defence outpost, its ultimate goal Australia itself. The battle was fought between this force and an American fleet waiting for it in the Coral Sea. Air attack from the American carriers drove the Japanese back to the north.

A month later the Japanese, frustrated in the south, struck east at Midway. Once again the Americans were waiting for them. The Japanese ships were sighted on June 3rd. Next day American carrier aircraft began a series of devastating attacks; by the evening the Japanese force was in full retreat, the sea covered with the smoke and wreckage of its burning carriers, battleships and cruisers.

MAKING FOR THE GREAT CARRIER YORKTOWN, JAPANESE BOMBERS WEAVE IN THROUGH HEAVY ANTI-AIRCRAFT FIRE IN THE BATTLE OF MIDWAY.

THROUGH A RISING STORM OF FIRE THE ATTACK IS PRESSED HOME. THE CARRIER IS HIT FULL ON HER FLIGHT DECK. SHE IS WRECKED.

THE GREAT SHIP IS DYING. THE VAST AND EMPTY DECK ROLLS OVER TOWARDS THE SEA. TORPEDOES STRUCK HER AS SHE STRUGGLED HOME.

Dauntless dive bombers go down to attack the Japanese fleet at Midway. Smoke from a burning enemy ship rises in a straight column in the still air. The American attacks on the Japanese fleet were made across several hundreds of miles of ocean by bombers from the carriers Enterprise, Hornet, and Yorktown, and by land-based planes from Midway. Losses of aircraft were heavy on both sides. From many attacks no aircraft returned. American air supremacy was established during the first two days and destructively exploited during the last two of the four-day battle. The Japanese fleet was estimated to have lost nine ships sunk, including four aircraft carriers, three battleships and four cruisers damaged, and 275 aircraft destroyed. Except for the Yorktown, American losses in ships were comparatively light.

TURRETS SPREADEAGLED BY BOMBS, A JAP CRUISER LIES DISABLED.

HOME FROM THE BATTLE, U.S. ARMY AIRMEN TELL THEIR STORIES.

Heaviest American loss in the Battle of the Coral Sea was the carrier Lexington, seen ablaze and sinking in these four pictures. From their abandoned ship men swarm down the ropes to the boats. A destroyer takes off the wounded.

The ship is shattered by a great explosion set off by fires started earlier in the day by direct hits from carrier-based Japanese bombers. One of the carrier's own aircraft is toppled over her stern by the blast of the explosion.

Burning along her length, the Lexington settles deep in the water. On the flight deck, to the right, her ranged aircraft are consumed in the fires. Beyond control, she has been ordered sunk by one of her attendant destroyers.

Not a living soul on board, under a pall of smoke, the carrier goes down like a blackened log. This was the final act in the first sea battle in which surface ships did not exchange a shot and carrier aircraft did all the killing.

2. THE CAMPAIGN IN NEW GUINEA

The enemy had reached the north coast of New Guinea in the last week of January 1942, landing at Lae, and later, Salamaua. By July he had worked down to Gona and Buna. Then he moved south and inland upon Port Moresby, the last remaining defence outpost before Australia. He crossed the Owen Stanley Range and came fast down the southern slopes towards the port and airfield. He was halted some 30 miles away from Moresby at Eoribaiwa Ridge. Simultaneously, a Japanese force landed at Milne Bay to advance upon Port Moresby from the east. It was beaten off. Against the huge background of the Pacific these seemed small events. But from this mark the Japanese tide in the S.W. Pacific was to rise no higher.

With the turn of the tide, the great north coast of the island, over 1,800 miles from tip to tip, took on a new significance. To the Allies on the defensive, it had been the last breakwater between the mainland of Australia and the flood of Japanese aggression. To the advancing Allies, it became MacArthur's main road back to the Philippines. The series of movements shown by the arrows on the map below traces the progress of the Australians and the Americans along that main road—from Port Moresby to Sansapor, and then across to Morotai in the Moluccas. It was a bitterly contested advance against entrenched and experienced enemies. It took almost exactly two years to accomplish—from September 1942 to September 1944. It is a measure of the advantage that lay with the aggressor in the Pacific that the Japanese had virtually overrun the island less than two months after Pearl Harbour.

The Allied offensive in New Guinea divides itself into two phases. There was firstly a period of slow and costly fighting against the main Japanese concentrations in the east of the island between Bogadjim and Buna. This is the area on the map covered by the many short and intertwining arrows. Of the two years of the Allied offensive, eighteen months were spent in fighting to break the Japanese power in this relatively small area. The Japanese were defeated in a series of three enveloping movements. The first of them ended in January 1943 when Buna fell to a combined Australian and American assault. There was then a long pause until mid-1943 when the advance was resumed in an enveloping movement around the next Japanese concentration at Lae and Salamaua. These two strongholds fell in September. Then in January-February 1944, the third and last envelopment began. The Americans landed at Saidor and the Australians pushed on from Finschhafen, trapping all the Japanese forces between them. Meanwhile, in the previous December, the Americans crossed the straits and landed in New Britain to threaten Rabaul. These movements closed the first phase of the New Guinea fighting.

In the second phase the speed of the advance was enormously increased. The long sweeping arrows stemming from the area of Saidor represent a series of seaborne landings by the Americans each one of which eliminated a Japanese base or outflanked a Japanese concentration. The first and biggest advance was the triple leap to Tanahmera Bay, Hollandia, and Aitape in April 1944. In May the Americans leaped forward on to Wakde. Ten days later they jumped another 200 miles to Biak. "For strategic purposes," said General MacArthur, "this marks the end of the New Guinea campaign." In early July the Americans went on to Noemfoor; in late July they reached the end of New Guinea at Sansapor. While the American role in this phase of the operations was to carry out these great amphibious leaps to the west, the Australians took over the hard and costly business of exterminating the by-passed garrisons. By the middle of 1944 they had cleared the coast to a point just east of Wewak.

In September the Americans gave vivid point to the strategic implication of the New Guinea campaign by leaping from the island's western point to Morotai, gaining a base only 300 miles from the Philippines. It had been a long hard road from Buna and Gona.

ARROWS TRACE TWO YEARS' HARD FIGHTING, SHOW THE 2,000-MILE ADVANCE FROM END TO END OF NEW GUINEA AND THEN THE LEAP TO MOROTAI.

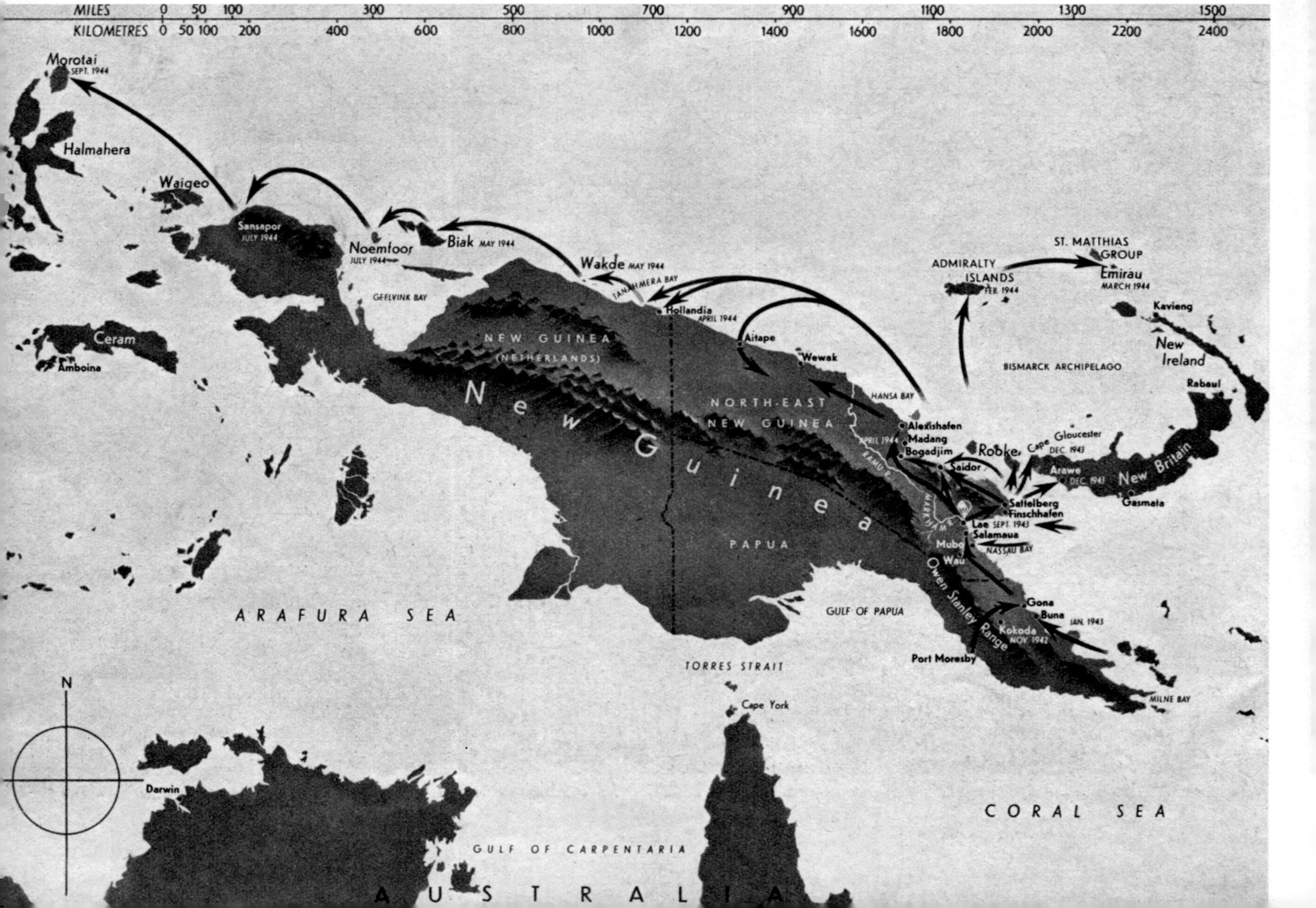

A QUEENSLAND CORPORAL SQUATS WITH HIS TOMMY-GUN IN THE LONG GRASS OUTSIDE GONA. THE JAPANESE ARE A HUNDRED YARDS AWAY.

ALONG THE FRESH-CUT ZIGZAGS OF THE KOKODA TRAIL 25-POUNDERS ARE HAULED INTO THE HEART OF THE JUNGLE FOR THE ATTACK ON BUNA.

THE ADVANCE ON BUNA AND GONA

When the Australians broke out from their narrow coastal strip at Port Moresby in September 1942, and fought their way back over the Owen Stanley Range towards Buna and Gona, they did three things. They inflicted upon the Japanese forces a lasting land defeat. They saved their own country from direct attack. They added to the records of fighting Australia a name as undying as Gallipoli—the steep, muddy, bloody Kokoda Trail. Once across it—Kokoda was recaptured on November 2nd—the Australians drove the Japanese northwards and downwards before them until they were pressed against the sea at Buna and Gona. Attacking with the Americans who had landed by air on the north coast, the Australians had taken both strongholds by January 1943. Losses were very heavy, and about the same on both sides. By the last week in January all Papua was clear of the enemy.

Over the crest of the Owen Stanleys, Australians thread down through the tropical forest across ravines spanned by felled trees.

Americans cross a river to join the Australians for the assault after landing on the coast to the east. Beauty of this scene is deceptive. Fighting conditions were everywhere terrible.

A LIGHT TANK BLASTS AT JAP DEFENCES BEFORE BUNA. A PILLBOX SMOKES AT LEFT. GROUND IS LITTERED WITH SHOT-DOWN PALM FRONDS

Two Australians shelter in the screen of high grass for a smoke. Below, Japanese wounded are tended as they lie on rough stretchers cut from the palms.

Wounded in the arm, an Australian is tended by comrades in a first aid post in a nest of grass. Below, Papuans carry casualties back to a dressing station.

An American patrol slops through mud and slush and rain-drenched forest towards the Papuan border. Rifles are at the ready. The last Japanese pockets, small harried parties of men retreating from Gona, are falling back upon their next bases, Lae and Salamaua. Rain was a deadly enemy to both sides throughout the campaign in New Guinea. It filled the rivers, soaked the camps, turned the jungle into swampland. Men fought two foes—the enemy and rain-bred disease.

LEAVING THE TRANSPORTS THAT FLEW THEM TO WAU, AUSTRALIANS GO STRAIGHT INTO ACTION. AIRFIELD IS UNDER ENEMY RIFLE FIRE

THE NOOSE ROUND LAE AND SALAMAUA

With Papua cleared, the next enemy bases in the path of the Allied offensive were Lae and Salamaua. A noose was dropped around them, and then drawn tight. This required a remarkable fourfold operation, shown on the map on page 12. Australians, marching overland, pressed down to the coast from Wau and Mubo. Americans landed in Nassau Bay below Salamaua. Then a combined American and Australian outflanking landing was made above Lae. Finally, the Japanese were taken in the rear by an airborne landing north of the two bases in the Markham Valley, the first ever to be made in the Pacific war. These operations were set in train in June 1943. Lae and Salamaua fell to the Australians nine weeks later.

GUNNERS REASSEMBLE THEIR 25-POUNDERS AFTER UNLOADING THEM FROM THE PLANES. THE ADVANCE FROM WAU WAS ENTIRELY AIR-SUPPLIED.

The Markham River landing is in progress in this magnificent photograph. American transport aircraft are dropping U.S. paratroops, Australian gunners and 25-pounders into the valley. They are flying very low against a billowing smoke screen. Picture shows how sharp was the jump. On the right men can be seen leaping from the incoming planes, their parachutes still unopened. To the left men dropped from the same point are touching the

ground. In the foreground lie parachutes discarded by troops already down. The smoke screen lies between the men and the Markham River. In the valley a party of Australian engineers kept a punctual rendezvous with the paratroops after a five days' climb over the craggy mountains seen beyond the river, bridged the stream, and built an airstrip. The purpose of the drop, on September 5th, 1943, was to block any escape of the Japanese in Lae and Salamaua

First line of the smoke screen to cover the Markham Valley landings is drawn across the flat and swampy river bed by Boston bombers. The paratroops are due to arrive in a few minutes.

After the landing the scrubby landscape is daubed with the white of hundreds of abandoned parachutes. Men, guns, planes are gone. Further down the Markham Valley the battle has opened.

DOWN A WAR-SWEPT TRACK AUSTRALIANS

MARCH INTO LAE, CAPTURED TWO DAYS EARLIER. LOWLAND HEAT AND DUST REPLACE THE MUD AND STEAM OF THE DRENCHED FORESTS.

Jap gunners can be seen crouched for protection inside the blast walls of their gun sites at Boram as American planes sweep low overhead. None of the six guns is firing. Beehive at right is the control position. The photograph was taken by the departing plane from which the delayed parachute bomb is falling.

Attacking bomber is on the point of releasing its load on a Japanese freighter lying at anchor at Wewak. The bomb spout still in the air on its port bow marks the miss of an outgoing bomber. On the far left a Jap ship is on fire

Given no rest, the last Japanese by bombers. Encirclement by land

Nine parachute bombs float down the runway of Boram airfield near Wewak. A fuel truck has halted directly in their path. Two planes lie wrecked at bottom left. An undamaged plane is drawn off the runway to the right. Earlier raids on the airfield broke the palm trees and tore the rain-filled craters.

base of Wewak is attacked yet again and raids by air made it useless.

Low-flying B.25s rove down the New Guinea coast searching out ships and airstrips. Burning in the centre are the buildings of Dagua airfield, cut by the Japanese from the coastal forest and provided with a small jetty for seaborne supplies.

LANDING CRAFT STREAK THROUGH STILL WATER INTO TANAHMERA BAY. THIS OPERATION ADVANCED THE NEW GUINEA FRONT BY OVER 400 MILES.

LEAP TO HOLLANDIA

The biggest assembly of land, sea, and air forces yet used in the South-West Pacific was set in motion in April 1944, for the triple landing at Aitape, Hollandia, and Tanahmera Bay. Dutch troops and Australian ships joined the Americans. This amphibious operation trapped the Japanese Eighteenth Army in a narrow belt of coast either side of Wewak. Similar leaps forward cleared the rest of New Guinea.

Crowded with troops, trucks, guns, and stores, a landing craft pushes in through the morning mist. Below, supplies are landed on Tanahmera beach. A rough track has been cut up through the undergrowth to the right.

Sherman tanks cluster for a mopping-up operation near Hollandia. Smoke comes from an enemy ammunition dump fired in the pre-landing bombardment. Below, American troops pass down the beach past derelict Jap supplies.

PARATROOPS FLOAT DOWN ON THE BEACHHEAD AT NOEMFOOR IN JULY 1944. THIS ADVANCE BROLGHT THE ALLIES TO NEW GUINEA'S WESTERN END.

A MASSIVE LINE OF LANDING SHIPS LIES AGAINST CAPE GLOUCESTER BEACH IN NEW BRITAIN. THE MEN POURING OUT ARE REINFORCEMENTS

FOR THE ASSAULT TROOPS NOW FIGHTING INLAND. INVASION OF NEW BRITAIN SECURED AIRFIELDS FOR THE CLOSER BOMBING OF RABAUL

A WARHAWK FIGHTER RACES PROTECTINGLY OVERHEAD AS THE FIRST WAVE OF AMERICAN ASSAULT TROOPS BREAKS OVER THE BEACH AT

The master purpose of the Solomons campaign was to paralyse Rabaul and Kavieng, the biggest enemy bases in the S.W. Pacific, and so protect the exposed northern flank of the Allied advance along the New Guinea coast towards the Philippines. The dated arrows show how this was achieved by February-March 1944.

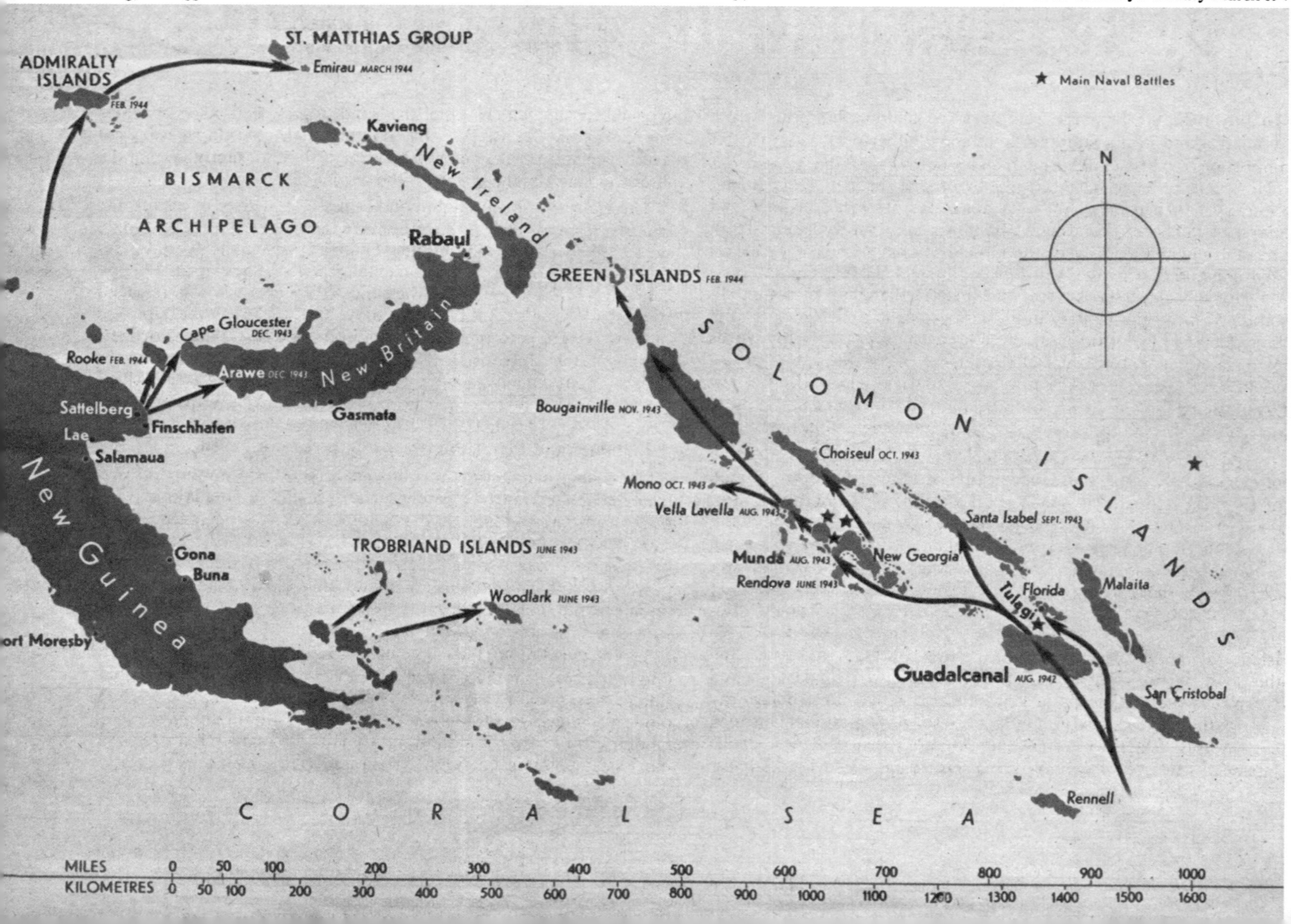

RENDOVA TOWARDS THE SHELTER OF THE TREES. THE LANDING, IN MID-1943, CARRIED THE SOLOMONS OFFENSIVE ON FROM GUADALCANAL.

3. THE CAPTURE OF THE SOLOMONS

In July 1942, the Japanese were observed building an airfield on a small island in the Southern Solomons, hitherto of no particular importance, called Guadalcanal. The meaning of the airfield was plain enough. Their defeats in the two battles of the Coral Sea and Midway had persuaded them to abandon the naval advance and revert to blitzkrieg—land-based bombing followed by assault landings. From the security of the airfield at Guadalcanal they meant to bomb and destroy the Allied bases in the New Hebrides and New Caledonia. These bases were vital links in the chain of communication between the United States and Australia and New Zealand. Since the defence of that line of communication was, in the words of the Commander-in-Chief of the United States Navy, a " must " of the Pacific war, it became a " must " to deal quickly with the new Guadalcanal airfield. It was decided to invade the island and capture the airfield. From this decision sprang the campaign of the Solomons.

An American force was gathered in New Zealand. On the morning of August 7th it landed on Guadalcanal and the neighbouring island of Florida. The airfield was captured by the next afternoon. For the next five months Guadalcanal was the storm centre of the South Pacific. Fighting raged in its jungles, and on the seas around it a series of naval battles was fought as the opposing fleets strove to reinforce and supply their struggling armies ashore. These naval battles, starred in the map on this page, cost both sides very heavily. For the Americans they had a disastrous beginning in the Battle of Savo Island two nights after the landing. Four cruisers were sunk ; and the loss shortly afterwards of the aircraft carriers Hornet and Wasp left the Americans in a position of actual naval inferiority during the next crucial months of struggle upon Guadalcanal. Despite this, American warships and aircraft defeated most of the Japanese attempts to bring in reinforcements during August-November, by which time the land forces had asserted their superiority in the island. By January 1943 the Japanese were overborne and on the night of February 7th-8th, exactly six months after the landing, the enemy withdrew his last troops.

The campaign in the Solomons began as a defensive move—the capture of an air base that would have threatened the Allied supply lines. Like the campaign in New Guinea it began slowly and painfully—six months to secure two small islands. But—again like the campaign in New Guinea—when the Allied advance was resumed in the middle of 1943 it began to move fast. Though the Japanese made every effort to retain their hold on the Central and Northern Solomons they lost all their positions one by one in the months between June and November 1943. In February 1944, the Allied forces moved a further step north-west when American and New Zealand troops occupied the Green Islands. At the same time the Admiralties and the St. Matthias group were occupied.

The change in tempo in the campaign in New Guinea was paralleled by a change in strategic meaning. Until the fall of Guadalcanal, the purpose of the fighting in the Solomons was the defence of the trans-Pacific supply line. But when the advance was resumed, its purpose was quite different. The supply line was secure ; and the purpose of the continuation of the advance from Guadalcanal was to defend the flank of the great westward advance in New Guinea. In a sense the north-western line of the Solomons leads nowhere. It peters out south of the equator. But it contained or passed alongside bases, notably Rabaul, from which the Japanese could threaten the precariously exposed line of supply for the New Guinea offensive, which *was* leading somewhere : to the Philippines. The landings in the Green and Admiralty Islands completed a swinging movement pivoting on New Guinea and guaranteeing its security.

American troops go in at Guadalcanal. Jap bombers are overhead. Cleared patch to the left is Henderson Field.

WEARY TROOPS UNLOAD THEIR BARGE IN STEAMY HEAT. IN THE FACES AND FIGURES OF THESE MEN IS WRITTEN THE STORY OF GUADALCANAL.

THE BATTLE OF GUADALCANAL

Guadalcanal, the first real offensive move in force in the Pacific, was a long, weary, bloody battle in which the issue hung precariously for many a long day and night. The landing was on August 7th, 1942. The outcome wavered for eight weeks, and it was another 15 before the Japanese were finally beaten out of the island. The prize in the Battle of Guadalcanal was a partly constructed airfield from which the Japanese had planned to prepare the way for a further big advance in the South Pacific. Renamed Henderson Field by the Americans, the struggle for it made it the most famous air base in the Pacific. Guadalcanal was two battles in one. It was a battle in dark jungles and swamps between land forces. It was a battle in the narrow sea defiles of the islands and in the open seas to the north and south between naval and air forces, each struggling to strengthen its own men and prevent the reinforcement of the enemy. Both battles were won. In neither was the margin large.

Roaring with flame and dead in the water the torpedoed Wasp sinks in the wide seas south of the Solomons. Tiny silhouetted figures on the flight deck, the last men leave her.

Landing craft loaded with New Zealanders head for the beaches of mountainous Vella Lavella. Empty boats thread their way back to the transports for more men. The ladder of the Solomons is now being ascended.

American troops stumble ashore at Rendova in a grey ra transports had been heavily bombed. Two hundred miles to

PATROL IN BOUGAINVILLE FORDS A STREAM CHOKED WITH DEBRIS OF SHELL-TORN TREES.

THE FLAME-THROWER SEEN IN THE PREVIOUS PICTU

CLIMBING THE RUNGS OF THE SOLOMONS

With the Japanese driven from the Southern Solomons, the next task was to climb north-west, island by island, until the Central and Northern Solomons were also clear. The most important enemy position in the Central Solomons was again an airfield : Munda, on New Georgia. On June 30th, 1943, the Americans landed on Rendova Island, to the south of the airfield. Four days later they invaded New Georgia itself. The airfield was captured on August 5th, one year less two days later than the

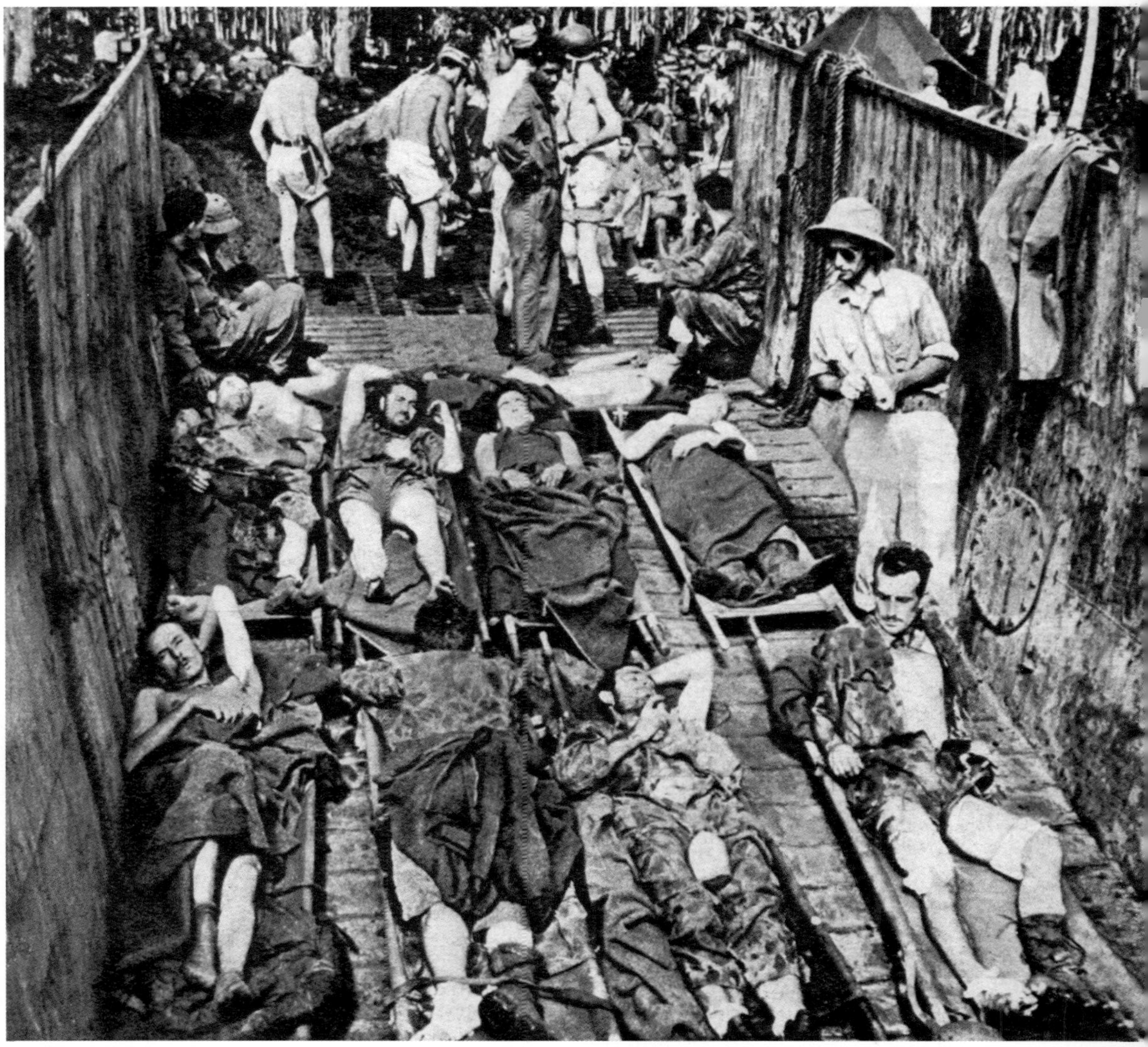

dawn and flop for breath behind the palm trees. Their
west of Guadalcanal, Rendova guarded a vital enemy airfield.

Wounded men from New Georgia lie restlessly in the oppressive heat in the landing barge that will take them to a base hospital. Most have got leg wounds from Japanese bullets in the battle for Munda airfield.

CHES A JAP FOXHOLE IN THE PATH OF THE PATROL.

LADEN MARINES LABOUR FORWARD TO THE BOUGAINVILLE FRONT THROUGH KNEE-DEEP MUD.

first landing on Guadalcanal. The fall of Munda was the climax in the Central Solomons. Vella Lavella, the next objective, was invaded on August 15th. By October 6th the Japanese had completed the evacuation of the Central Solomons. Late that month the New Zealanders went into the Treasuries, and Choiseul, east of New Georgia, was occupied. There remained Bougainville, the large northernmost island of the Solomons. On November 1st, there were several landings on the island, all of them in Empress Augusta Bay. By November 8th the beachheads were consolidated. The fighting on the island was heavy. The encirclement of all the Jap forces left in the Solomons was completed by the occupation of the Green Islands on February 14th, 1944.

Small bitter battle is fought to the death in the dense Bougainville jungle. Hidden Japs have mined the tank and shot the commander, lying crumpled beside it. Tensely, Marines are hunting them.

RABAUL BURNS AT THE HEIGHT OF A LOW-LEVEL BOMBING ATTACK. STORES AND WAREHOUSES SMOKE ALONG THE WATER-FRONT OF THE

RABAUL DIES ON THE VINE

Centrally placed at the eastern tip of the arc of N
Britain, protected against storm and invasion by
curved shield of New Ireland, Rabaul became

ENEMY WARSHIPS SURPRISED AT ANCHOR IN RABAUL HARBOUR SCATTER AND MAKE FOR THE OPEN SEA AS TORPEDO AND DIVE-BOMBERS FR

SE. IN THE FOREGROUND A B.25 MEDIUM BOMBER RACES OVER A JAPANESE FREIGHTER. OTHER BOMBERS ARE STILL COMING IN.

at enemy base in the South-West Pacific. It fell the Japanese on January 23rd, 1942, less than en weeks after the attack on Pearl Harbour. Two years later it was dying on the vine. The scissors of which one blade was the advance in the Solomons and the other the invasion of western New Britain and the Admiralties (map, p. 28) had severed every stem by which the sap could reach it. Then it was laid waste by carrier-borne and land-based planes.

AMERICAN TASK FORCE SWEEP DOWN UPON THEM IN THE HEAVY ATTACK OF NOVEMBER 5th, 1943. SIX OF THEM ARE ALREADY ON FIRE.

CATALINAS PATROL THE WASTES OF AMCHITKA OVER THE WINDSWEPT TENTS OF THE U.S. LANDING FORCE.

4. FAR NORTH: THE ALEUTIANS

In the fogs and storms of the extreme North Pacific lies the Aleutian chain. Its islands are stepping stones between Alaska and the Japanese Kuriles (map, pp. 4-5). It is the shortest route from North America to Japan. But it is also the worst. Thick fogs enshroud it. Violent winds toss the seas, making all operations precarious. Winter storms rage out of the storm factory of the Bering Sea at the rate of one or two a week. In this forbidding theatre the war moves have been few. The Japanese occupied Kiska and Attu in a June fog in 1942. The Americans blocked them by occupying Adak in August and Amchitka, near Kiska, in January 1943. In May they landed in Attu, clearing the island after bitter fighting. In August the American and Canadian invaders of Kiska found that the last Japanese in the Aleutians had slipped away in the mist.

ALONG A RAMP OF EARTH AND STONES AMERICANS UNLOAD STORES ON THE HARSH BEACH OF KISKA.

THIN LINE OF AMERICANS

THREADS THE BLACK SIDE OF A SNOW-PATCHED MOUNTAIN ON ATTU. THE PATROL IS MOVING AGAINST ONE OF THE LAST ENEMY POCKETS

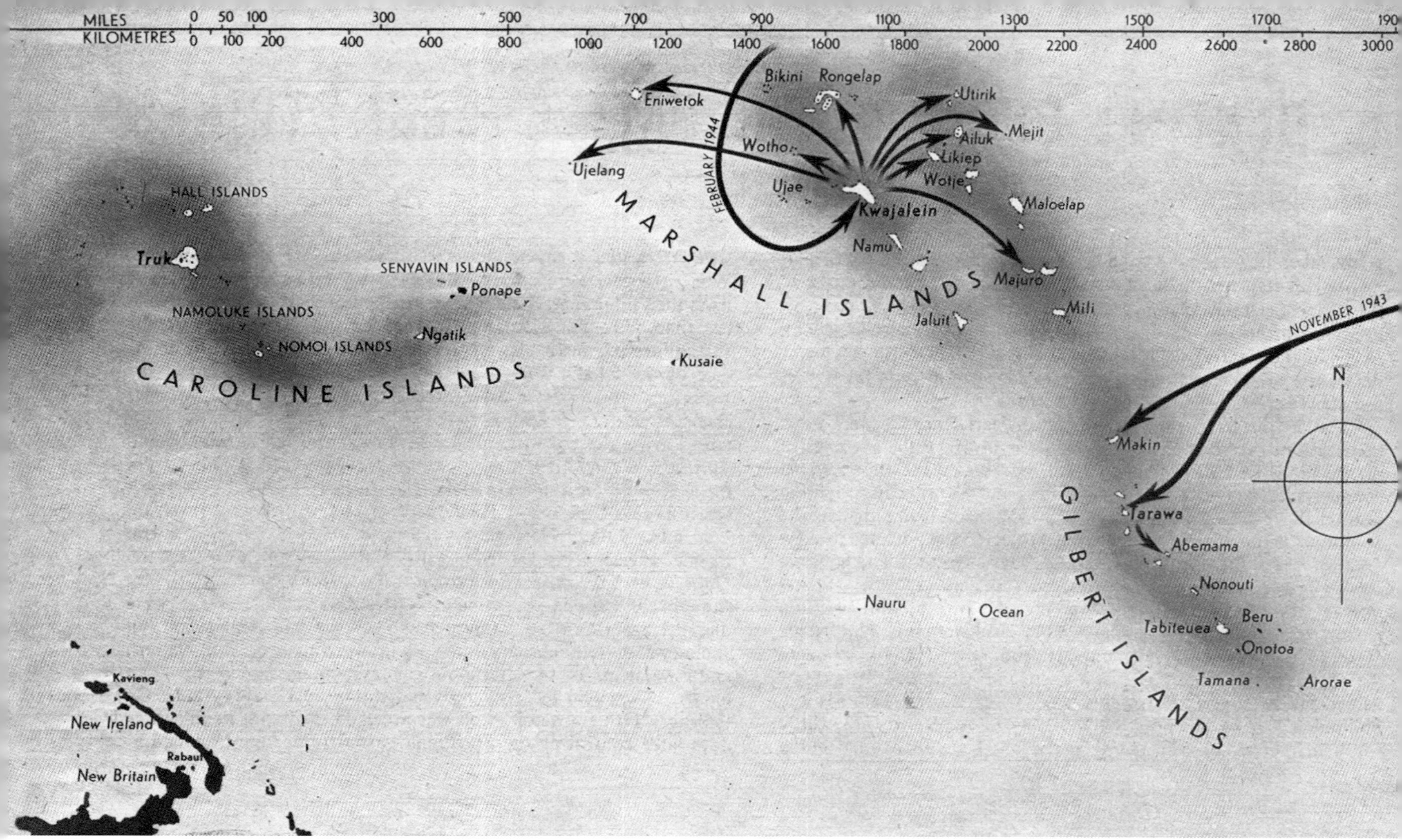

START OF THE CENTRAL PACIFIC OFFENSIVE WAS THE LANDING IN THE GILBERTS. INVADED NEXT WERE THE JAPANESE MARSHALLS, 500 MILES ON.

5. CENTRAL PACIFIC: THE BATTLE FLEET STRIKES

November 1943 saw the opening of a new phase in the ocean war. For in that month the United States Fleet, with the losses of Pearl Harbour more than made good, moved out from its Hawaiian bases to reassert its authority over the Pacific. That reassertion took shape in the Central Pacific offensive (map, pages 4-5), which was finally to interlock with the southern offensive at a point within assault range of the Philippines.

Once the disastrous few months after Pearl Harbour were over, there was no phase of the Allied offensive in which the presence of the Pacific Fleet had not been felt. It had halted the Japanese sea conquests in the Battles of the Coral Sea and of Midway. Fighting against superior forces, it managed to make the campaign in the Solomons possible. It sustained and protected the advance in New Guinea. But these advances in the South-Western Pacific were predominantly land-air operations, with the naval forces supplementing them. The Central Pacific offensive was predominantly a naval-air operation, with supplementary land support. The Pacific Fleet, in undertaking it, was moving from the wings to dominate the centre of the stage. Manifesting an unrivalled power, it threw its weight in a great drive due west from Hawaii towards the Philippines. It sought no circuits or by-passes. It swerved a little south first of all to take the Gilberts, but from then on it cut a straight swathe through the heart of the Japanese island empire. When it began in November 1943, it was fighting 3,400 miles away from the Philippines. Less than a year later, it had established bases less than 500 miles away, and its carrier planes were bombing the Philippines regularly. Its advance of 3,000 miles had changed the face of the Pacific war.

For this great naval drive across the Central Pacific the first essential was the recapture of the Gilberts, a group of coral atolls lying across the equator. The attack was directed at Makin and Tarawa. The landings took place on November 20th. Makin fell the next day after a sharp brief struggle, but on Tarawa the bloodiest small battle of the whole Pacific had to be fought before it fell on November 24th. Next across the route selected for the Central Pacific offensive lay the Marshalls, 500 miles north-west of the Gilberts, and the outermost rampart of Japan's island empire. On January 30th the largest offensive operations yet undertaken were directed against them. Majuro was occupied without fighting on January 31st. On February 2nd landings were made on Roi, Namur, and Kwajalein. By the afternoon Roi and Namur were in American hands. Kwajalein fell after heavier fighting on February 5th. On February 17th Eniwetok Atoll was attacked, and with its fall three days later control of the Marshalls passed into American hands.

Carriers and battleships of the Pacific Fleet striking force lie majestically at anchor in the captured Marshalls.

TARAWA

This is the waterfront of famous Tarawa, quiet now, an inferno of battle a few hours earlier. At this point the full fury of the American assault had broken upon it in a wave of steel and men. The landing was fiercely resisted. Dead men float in the water under the track of the landing craft aground on the right, and lie under the sea wall where they were shot down. An amphibious landing craft has

piled itself up on the bank of coconut logs which it was trying to climb. To its left is a half sunken blockhouse, now wrecked, once hidden in the grove of desolate trees. As they came in to Tarawa, the marines' landing craft mostly stuck on unexpected reefs 300 yards out. Unfaltering, they waded methodically in through a sea raked with fire from the beach ahead where alone a landing was possible and where the Japanese garrison of 3,500 men was concentrated. The troops attacking Makin were also stopped on reefs. The cover of this book shows them wading in towards the waiting enemy.

FROM THE RIBBON-THIN BEACHHEAD AT TARAWA MARINES RUSH THE OUTER PALISADE. PHOTOGRAPH WAS TAKEN FROM THE WATER EDGE.

AN ENEMY PILLBOX IS SURROUNDED. A GROUP OF MARINES IS ABOUT TO BREAK IN. OUTER CIRCLE OF MEN WATCHES FOR FUGITIVES.

MARINES FIGHT BEHIND ROUGHLY PILED SANDBAGS IN THE HEART OF THE DEFENCES. STRIPPED PALMS ADD THEIR FAMILIAR PATTERN.

THE MOUND OF WRECKAGE WHERE THE MARINES ARE CONVERGED IS A CAPTURED STRONGPOINT. THE BATTLE ENDS IN A RUINED ISLAND.

IN THIS TERRIBLE PHOTOGRAPH OF WAR, DEAD JAPANESE LIE SPRAWLED ON THE HUGE SLOPE OF A WRECKED BLOCKHOUSE. MORE DEAD LIE IN A

HEAP AMONG THE UPROOTED PALMS. THESE VAST BLOCKHOUSES OF CEMENT, LOGS, AND PILED SAND WERE THE FORTRESSES OF TARAWA.

A SYMBOLIC FIST OF SMOKE IS RAISED BY BOMBED ENEMY ISLET IN THE MARSHALLS. THE QUICKENING OFFENSIVE HAS REACHED JAPANESE SOIL.

THE ONSLAUGHT ON THE MARSHALL ISLANDS

The invasion of the Marshalls was preceded by a bombardment of unparalleled power. The lesson of Tarawa, where the defences half-survived the shelling and bombing, was applied with overwhelming force. Battleships and aircraft were assembled in the largest striking force yet used. Over 14,000 tons of shells and bombs fell on Roi and Namur alone. In all, perhaps half the defenders were killed. American casualties were correspondingly lighter: 286 killed up to the fall of Kwajalein compared with 8,122 Japanese dead.

Flight deck men of an American carrier throw themselves flat as an enemy torpedo bomber races toward the ship. Shells are bursting low in its path. The carrier was part of a Task Force moving in to bomb and shell the Marshalls.

Plane is hit at close quarters before its attack is delivered. Flame and smoke spurt from the underside of the port wing where a shell has struck home. The deliberate helmeted men in the well at the side of the deck are gunners.

The plane lurches towards the sea, its port wing now lopped off. Clearly seen, the torpedo drops harmlessly away under the eddying train of flame from the wing stub.

LOW-LEVEL PHOTOGRAPH FROM A SUPPORT PLANE SHOWS THE INVASION OF ENIWETOK IN PROGRESS. AMPHIBIOUS TANKS CHURN IN AND

MOUNT THE BEACH. TROOPS ARE MAKING THEIR WAY ACROSS THE STRICKEN WASTE THAT WAS ONCE A WAVING COCONUT GROVE.

FIRE IS SWEEPING THIS AIRFIELD ON KWAJALEIN AS AMERICAN TANKS STEER PAST CRATERS TOWARDS THE JAPANESE ENTRENCHED IN

THE CURVE OF TREES AROUND THE PERIMETER. THREE MORE TANKS ARE IN ACTION BY THE COLLAPSED AIRCRAFT ON THE RIGHT.

On Namur, marines move up to the front along a trench cut by the Japanese and then abandoned. The fighting on Namur lasted less than one day against defenders dazed by heavy air and sea bombardment.

Shell-wrecked pillbox on Kwajalein is cautiously approached by marines crouching in the devastation caused by the bombardment. The fall of Kwajalein came after three days' hard fighting.

Victory morning on Kwajalein.

CARRIER PLANES OF A JOINT BRITISH AND AMERICAN NAVAL FORCE FORM UP IN THE EARLY MORNING SKY FOR THE ATTACK ON SOERABAJA.

6. CLOSING IN: THE PHILIPPINES

IT was now the middle of 1944, and the stage was largely set for the culminating invasion of the Philippines. It was the eve of fulfilment. Guadalcanal and Tarawa, Makin and Kwajalein, the Kokoda Trail and Buna, Lae and the Hollandia landings—all these, as the first American assault craft grated on the eastern beaches of Leyte on October 19th, were to fall into their place in a pattern the world could see.

Once the Marshalls had fallen, the Pacific Fleet had been roaming the Central Pacific almost at will. Meanwhile, in New Guinea, the Allied land forces had reached the western tip of the island. But before the converging naval forces of the Central Pacific and the land forces of New Guinea could join hands for the concerted assault on the Philippines, three final touches to the master plan were necessary. Firstly, the Central Pacific forces must capture the Japanese bases in the Marianas (map on this page), from which the right flank of the advance upon the Philippines could otherwise be endangered. Secondly, they must take the main points of the Palau Islands to form their own advanced base for the invasion. Thirdly, the New Guinea forces must leap westward from the island upon Morotai, both to give themselves an advanced base and to remove any enemy threat to the left or southern flank of the invasion of the Philippines.

By the end of September these moves had been successfully carried out. On June 15th, Allied forces landed on Saipan, capturing it by July 8th. Then Tinian quickly fell. On July 20th, the Americans landed on Guam, clearing it of the enemy by August 10th. On September 15th, the Central Pacific forces made their first landings on the Palau Islands, and on the same day the forces from New Guinea landed on Morotai. The fingertips of the Fleet in the north and the land forces in the south were now touching. Their hands were about to lock.

On October 19th, acting as a combined force, they invaded the Philippines. The rendezvous foreseen two years before had been kept. The two forces were essential complements for the operation. When the Fleet reached the Philippines it would need the co-operation of large land forces to deal with the great and waiting Japanese garrison. It would need General MacArthur—and MacArthur was there. But he would need, as in New Guinea he had not directly needed, the co-operation of large naval and naval-air forces, for otherwise his transports and landing craft could be attacked at sea and his invaders blockaded once they were ashore. He would need Admiral Nimitz—and Nimitz was there. The land forces had taken the land road by New Guinea, the sea forces the sea road across the Pacific. They had begun their interrelated drives thousands of miles apart, MacArthur in Queensland, Nimitz in the Hawaiian Islands. The Japanese could hardly have dreamed they would meet together in the seas lapping the eastern shores of the Philippines. But so it was.

The invasion of the Philippines was much the largest event of the Pacific War, and, once complete, it brings one phase of the war to an end. But here it is wise to distinguish just where this blow lands on the body of Japanese imperialism, and what it accomplishes of itself. The capture of the Philippines must be a mortal blow to the Japanese overseas empire. From them can be severed the main artery of communications to every territory outside Japan and Japanese-held China—to Burma and Malaya no less than to Java and Sumatra. No new force can flow into those extremities of Japanese conquest unless the Japanese can complete their overland route from North China to Siam. But it is not a blow that lands either on Japan itself or Japanese-held China. Fortress Japan remains fortress Japan, and the riches of much of China remain available for the great garrison. And the great garrison itself, spread through Japan and over much of China, and the main Japanese battle fleet, are still intact, awaiting the offensive which the forces of the United States and the British Commonwealth and Empire will share together.

THE OFFENSIVE SWEEPS IN UPON JAPAN FROM THE VASTNESS OF THE PACIFIC. HEAVY ARROWS ARE INVASIONS, LIGHT ARROWS RAIDS.

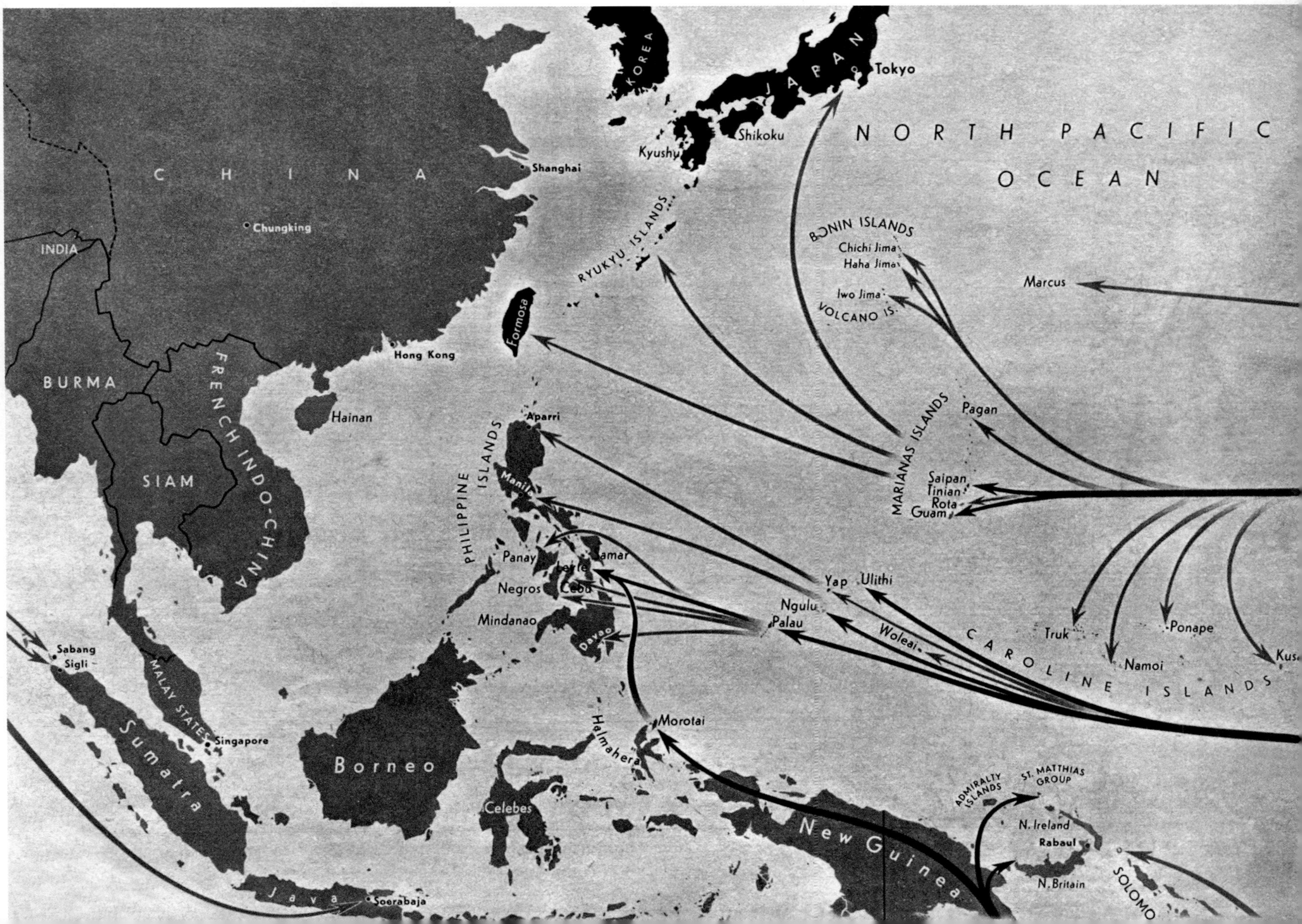

TWILIGHT SKY IS PITTED WITH SHELL BURSTS AS THE SILHOUETTED TASK FORCE BEATS AWAY JAP PLANES IN THE BATTLE OF THE MARIANAS.

INSIDE THE ISLAND WALL: THE MARIANAS

Deep inside the vast ring of islands forming the outer defences of Japan lie the Marianas, 1,500 miles almost due south of Tokyo. The main bases were attacked in June 1944, captured by August. The battle on Saipan against the Japanese garrison of 30,000 became the biggest single land battle of the Central Pacific, raging grimly and bloodily for twenty-five days. The invasion of the Marianas also brought about the biggest naval battle since Midway two years before. Powerful units of the Japanese fleet attempted to attack and beat away the invasion forces. Brought to battle in the open seas between Saipan and Luzon (map on pages 4-5) they were defeated in the Battle of the Marianas on June 19-20.

UNDER AIR ATTACK THE ENEMY FLEET SEEKING TO STEM THE SAIPAN INVASION EVASIVELY BREAKS LINE OF BATTLE AND TURNS FOR HOME.

FACE INTENT, BATTLE-GRIMED, A HOSPITAL CORPSMAN IN THE FRONT LINE AT SAIPAN DRIPS BLOOD PLASMA INTO A WOUNDED MAN.

D-DAY AT PELELIU

The whole dramatic pattern of the invasion of Peleliu, in the Palaus, is seen in this superb aerial photograph, taken on September 15th, 1944. In the distance, smoke billows from the shore where enemy installations have been set ablaze in the pre-invasion attack by bombers and warships of the Pacific Fleet. Closest inshore, in line abreast, lie rocket-firing landing ships, their positions marked by large puffs of

white smoke as they lay down a barrage to clear the beach of whatever has survived the Fleet bombardment. About to pass through them towards the shore are two long waves of cannon-armed amphibious tanks, the alligators. These will absorb the first counter-blows the enemy may be able to offer. Finally come the lines of troop-landing craft, chugging in with the first assault forces, fanning out wide wakes behind them. With the clarity of a diagram, this action photograph shows in their full development the technique and the material equipment of Pacific invasion perfected by the advancing Americans.

1. IT IS TEN MINUTES BEFORE ZERO HOUR AT PELELIU. THE ROCKET SHIPS WAIT. TROOP CARRIERS FORM UP BEHIND THE BATTLESHIPS.

3. CLUSTER UPON CLUSTER, THE ROCKETS RAIN DOWN. THE BACK DROP OF BLACK SMOKE IS THE RESULT OF THE FLEET BOMBARDMENT.

5. THE ASSAULT SIGNAL COMES. THE AMPHIBIOUS TANKS STREAM OUT FROM THE COVER OF THE BIG SHIPS TOWARDS THE SHROUDED SHORE.

THE ASSAULT ON MAKIN ISLAND

From the summit of a ridge wrested from the Japanese on Peleliu, marines gaze through the dark storm of continuing battle.

2. THE WORD IS GIVEN, AND THE ROCKET SHELLS BEGIN TO POUR ON TO THE BURNING BEACHES FROM THE DECKS OF THE LANDING CRAFT.

4. THE BARRAGE ROARS TO A CLIMAX. THE ROCKET SHIPS, STILL FIRING, GO CLOSER IN. A BATTLESHIP ADDS ITS HEAVY FIRE AT LEFT.

6. THE PELELIU LANDING HAS SUCCEEDED, AND TWO DAYS LATER THE SAME FIERCE SCENE BEGINS AGAIN OFF THE ISLAND OF ANGAUR.